forty

devotions for lent

Kory Plockmeyer

FAITH ALIVE®
Christian Resources

Grand Rapids, Michigan

Forty: Devotions for Lent, © 2012 by Faith Alive Christian Resources, 2850 Kalamazoo Ave. SE, Grand Rapids, Michigan, 49560.

ISBN 978-1-59255-723-3

10 9 8 7 6 5 4 3 2 1

FSC www.fsc.org MIX Paper from responsible sources FSC® C011935

Introduction

I hope that you will find these next forty-six days an opportunity to reflect upon and rest in the greatness of our God and the sacrifice of Jesus.

Lent is a time of fasting and mourning, remembering our sinfulness in light of the glory of Easter. It is a time to prepare our hearts for the coming of Easter Sunday.

Traditionally, the Sundays of Lent are miniature Easters—reminders in the middle of our fasting and reflection that we are looking forward to the glorious hope of the resurrection of Jesus.

One of the great images of preparation scattered throughout the Bible is a number: forty. Again and again, God's people spend periods of forty days or years waiting for an encounter with God. In this devotional, in keeping with the spirit of Lent and the celebration of Sunday mornings, each week will follow a different biblical story of such preparation. On Sundays, we will reflect on the good news of God to which each story points.

Grace and peace to all as we join our hearts in prayerful reflection this Lenten season.

—KP

DIRTY

"My ears had heard of you but now my eyes have seen you. Therefore I despise myself and repent in dust and ashes."

Read
Job 42:1-6

When I was a college student I went to a school that held an annual Ash Wednesday chapel service. Every year, I would see students walking across campus with what looked like a dirty smudge on their foreheads. To be honest, I avoided chapel that day each year. I wasn't sure I wanted somebody putting ashes on my forehead. It just seemed, well, dirty.

In today's reading, God has just finished speaking to Job, telling him that it is not his place to question the plans and ways of God. Job 38:1 tells us that God spoke to Job out of a storm. The encounter is so overwhelming, so breathtaking, that Job is nearly left speechless. Job has been brought face to face with a God who is so much bigger, so much more powerful, so much more awe-inspiring than Job could possibly have imagined. The only thing that Job can do in response is to get dirty—a sign of repentance and a symbol that he is not worthy of the God he has just encountered.

Sometimes, we forget just how big God is. We confine God to being the god who agrees with us, the god who is there as our "insurance policy," the god whom we encounter only when we're with the right people or singing the right songs. We cut God out of our professional and personal lives, believing that somehow these are domains outside God's dominion.

Lent brings us face to face with a God whose plans are bigger than anything we could have possibly imagined. At Lent we meet Jesus and discover a plan for salvation that includes death on a cross. During Lent, we encounter a God who loves us more than we can possibly imagine, a God who is more wonderful than we can know. Lent connects us to the God who is God of our good days and our bad, God of all times and places.

The only thing we can do in response is to get dirty.

PRAYER

Spend some time reflecting on the greatness of God. Consider ways in which you may have tried to put God into a box. Bring these things before God in confession. Then marvel at the majesty of God's love for us embodied in Jesus.

God, you are greater than our words can say and more wonderful than we can know. Forgive us for those times when we try to make you less than what you are. Help us to use this time of Lent to reflect on you and the majesty of your plans. Thank you for the grace you have given us in Jesus. Amen.

SO

> "So make yourself an ark of cypress wood; make rooms in it and coat it with pitch inside and out."
>
> **Read**
> Genesis 6:9-22

I love the word "so." Our entire world can change by the inflection given to this one little word.

A child comes home after curfew and walks through the door to find her mother standing in the kitchen. The mother says, "So."

A nervous young man finally works up the courage to ask a girl on a date. She thinks for a few moments. The young man swallows the lump in his throat: "So?"

God tells Noah that the world is corrupt and there will be a giant flood: "So."

When I read the story of Noah I feel as though God is so matter-of-fact. God has just given Noah the biggest news in world history and says, simply, "So make yourself an ark." As God describes the ark, the magnitude of Noah's problem becomes even greater. This isn't just any old building project. This is a small cruiseliner-sized project. God doesn't exactly beat around the bush. He just tells Noah, "So make yourself an ark."

During Lent we encounter a God of big plans. We encounter a God who comes to us with life-changing news and says to us, simply, "So."

Over the next forty-plus days, we will meet God again and again in unexpected ways and be given the opportunity to respond by building an ark. Maybe the ark will be the chance to go out of your way to help someone. The ark might be a chance to show love to a friend who is going through a rough patch in life. It may even be a call to a new job, a new city, or a new school.

God didn't stop with the instruction to Noah to build an ark. God doesn't leave Noah high and dry, hoping that everything will be okay. God promises to make a covenant with Noah and to protect him.

As we hear God's call on our lives, as we encounter God at work and school, as we connect with one another in relationship, with a promise of protection God says to us, simply, "So."

PRAYER

Take some time to quiet your heart before God. Spend a few moments resting in God's presence.

God, you have created the heavens and the earth. You call us to your work and equip us for the job. You bring us to a need and you promise us your blessing. Help us discern your voice from all the voices around us. Prepare our hearts to hear your directions, whether they be big or small, life-changing or natural, easy or hard. Amen.

SHUT

"The animals going in were male and female of every living thing, as God had commanded Noah. Then the LORD shut him in."

Read
Genesis 7:11-24

I am not much of a woodworker. My father, on the other hand, is extraordinarily talented with any sort of tool. He is somehow able to visualize a finished product with all its complexities, paying attention to the smallest detail. The evidence of his craftsmanship is hidden inside: nail heads tucked away where you can't see them, joints bound together seamlessly. If you asked each of us to build a boat, I can tell you whose boat I would trust to be leak-free.

When we encounter Noah in this passage, the ark is finally finished. The size is right. It has the right number of doors and windows. It's coated with pitch inside and out. Every last detail is in place. But in verse 16 we read something rather unexpected: "Then the Lord shut him in."

After months, maybe even years, of planning, preparation, and building, the storms are finally coming. But, ultimately, it's not Noah's handiwork that protects him from the floodwaters. It's not the pitch that will keep the boat from leaking. God finishes the task. I like to imagine

God locking the door and spreading pitch into all the cracks Noah missed.

Sometimes it's easy for us to feel overwhelmed when we consider the work to which God has called us. Sometimes we don't know where to begin or where to go next. We can feel lost, wondering why God has called us to this task. We look at other people and we feel unworthy, thinking that God can't possibly use someone like us. We face challenges at work and school and we begin to question our calling: "I feel like I'm failing at my job. Is this really where God is calling me?" "I'm trying my hardest, but it just doesn't seem good enough. Am I really cut out for this?"

God doesn't call us to offer perfectly completed tasks. Instead, we are called to faithfully follow where God leads us. When the floodwaters come, God is the one who completes our work. God takes our incomplete and imperfect offerings and brings them to perfection, shutting us in and protecting us from the storm.

PRAYER

Do you ever feel like your best isn't good enough? Where might God be leading you?

God, where we are weak, you are strong. When the storms of life rage around us, you protect us. You take our incomplete and imperfect works and rejoice in the offering. You complete the tasks we are unable to do. Guide us and protect us as we seek to follow your voice. Amen.

WAITING

> "By the first day of the first month . . . the water had dried up from the earth. By the twenty-seventh day of the second month the earth was completely dry."
>
> **Read**
> Genesis 8:13-22

Nobody likes impatient drivers. They're the ones who whip past you on the highway in the middle of a snowstorm. They're the ones who drive as far as possible before merging in a construction zone, the ones who drive over curbs and sidewalks to create a right turn lane even when there isn't one. They're the drivers who have no patience for waiting at stop lights because they feel a pressing weight to get somewhere as soon as possible.

People today have a hard time with patience. Most of us hate waiting: waiting for news about a house, waiting for decisions from the graduate schools we applied to, waiting for health, waiting for direction.

Noah's voyage at sea finally comes to an end after forty days of rain, one hundred fifty days at sea, forty days of resting on the mountain, and fourteen days between birds. Finally the world is livable again! Noah throws the covering off the ark, breathes in the fresh air, and . . . waits almost two months. Only when God says it's OK to leave do Noah and his family exit the ark.

We often wish that God's direction and guidance would come overnight. We hope that things will be different tomorrow. We keep waiting for God to make a career choice clear to us even though we feel no guidance. Some of us are looking for somebody to love, some of us are trying to have children, some of us are trying to find a job. It feels like all we do is wait, and we're sick of waiting.

Sometimes the waiting seems unbearable. Sometimes, like Noah, we wait with dry ground in clear sight. And sometimes every sign of hope is followed by more waiting. But God is faithful and good and promises to call us out of the ark.

When the rains seem as if they're never going to stop, when all we see around us is a never-ending sea of problems, even when it feels as though we're closed in and have no way out, we can remember that a rainbow is coming. We trust and wait for the day when God says, "Come out of the ark."

PRAYER

Are you waiting for anything in your life right now? In what areas do you have the most difficulty waiting for God's direction?

God, we are an impatient people. We frequently tire of waiting for you to reveal your will to us. Grant us the strength for the journey and the patience to bear with one another in love as we seek your guidance. Thank you for the promise that you are with us. Amen.

PINKY SWEAR

"I establish my covenant with you: Never again will all life be destroyed by the waters of a flood . . . This is the sign of the covenant I have established between me and all life on earth."

Read
Genesis 9:8-17

A signed piece of paper. Two children intertwining pinky fingers. A handshake. A nod of the head. Two simple words: "I promise."

Our life is based on a series of promises. We and our employers sign contracts as mutual promises of hard work and respect. We sign checks as a promise that the money we say is in the given account really is there. We exchange rings as a sign of a lifelong commitment. We go through each day trusting that the people around us will keep the promises they have made to us.

We are all too familiar, however, with the fact that people often fail to keep their promises. A secret told in confidence to a friend turns into a vicious rumor. Working conditions fail to match what we were promised. Promises of lifelong love turn into infidelity. Promises made don't always become promises kept.

In Genesis 9 we encounter the first example of God entering into a covenant. God makes a promise to Noah, his family, and all creation. God invites Noah and his family to enter into a relationship with him. And, in case they ever forget about this promise, God makes the rainbow into a symbol of the promise. After all of the rain and all of the trouble Noah and his family went through, God is still there.

When we are surrounded by so many broken promises, it can be easy to become cynical. The hope of the story of Noah, however, is that God is faithful forever. Sometimes we can be so saturated with stories like this that we fail to miss just how amazing this good news is.

When we feel abandoned by our friends, God is there. When we feel like we can't trust anyone, God is there. When we feel left out, the victim of one more broken promise, God is still there.

And in case we ever forget, God's beautiful light shines through after the rain. I like to think of it as a heavenly "pinky swear."

PRAYER

Reflect for a few moments on the people who have hurt you in the past. What broken promises remain with you today? How does God's faithfulness heal these pains?

God, we are a fickle people, prone to make promises and then break our word. Thank you for being faithful and for inviting us to enter into a covenant relationship with you. Help us to never lose sight of the majesty and beauty of your faithfulness. Amen.

FIRE

"To the Israelites the glory of the LORD looked like a consuming fire on top of the mountain. Then Moses entered the cloud as he went up on the mountain. And he stayed on the mountain forty days and forty nights."

Read Exodus 24:12-18

In a famous scene in C. S. Lewis' *The Lion, the Witch, and the Wardrobe*, Mr. Beaver describes the book's Christ-figure—the lion Aslan: "Safe? Who said anything about safe? But he is good. He's the King, I tell you." While Aslan is certainly "not a tame lion," he is nevertheless good, and those who love him entrust their lives to him.

In today's reading we are presented with a surprising juxtaposition of what is happening on Mount Sinai. The Israelites, down on the ground, see nothing when they look up but a consuming fire. Moses, on the mountain, enters into the cloud and spends forty days and forty nights with God. Moses gives up any idea of his own safety, trusting in God as he enters into God's presence on the mountaintop.

Some people look at God today and see only the consuming fire. They see a God who asks everything of them, demanding every last aspect of their lives. They see a God who changes the way they think, the way they talk, the way they treat others, and the way they spend their time. They look at so-called "Christian" behaviors and think that the

Christian life seems like a lot of work and not a lot of fun. They stand on the ground and see only the consuming fire of God.

When we commit ourselves to Jesus and enter into a relationship with him, we find that we have, indeed, walked straight into the cloud on top of the mountain. We enter the consuming fire and give up every last aspect of who we are to God. But we recognize the incomprehensible goodness of God. We recognize that even though God is not safe, God is good and God is King. We give up any idea of our own safety, trusting in God as we enter into God's presence wherever we are.

God invites us to enter the cloud. Will you give your life to God's consuming fire?

PRAYER

Reflect for a few moments on the people you know who see only the consuming fire and not the goodness of God. Pray for them specifically by name.

God, you are a consuming fire that takes every aspect of who we are and refines it. Help us to give up control and enter your presence. We pray for those who look on you only from a distance and see only a consuming fire. Move in their hearts and work through us as we seek to bring them into your presence. Amen.

DWELL

"Then have them make a sanctuary for me, and I will dwell among them."

Read
Exodus 25:1-9

When you live in an apartment complex, you get used to people coming and going. We have been living in our current apartment for about eight months, and in that time we have seen five different neighbors move into the apartments around us. Sometimes we come home and see the telltale signs that somebody has moved out: a balcony is suddenly empty, the window shades are always closed, the welcome mat is gone, and the things outside that personalized the apartment have moved on with the tenants. A couple of months later, the replacement of those items tells us that we have neighbors once more.

We use things like doormats, bird feeders, patio furniture, and window treatments to help make a house "home." These are the signs that mark a place as ours and help distinguish our apartment from any of the others in our building.

In today's reading, God tells Moses to receive offerings from the people to construct a tabernacle, a tent where God will dwell with the people of Israel. In the subsequent chapters, God gives Moses details on exactly how to build this tabernacle and all of its accompanying furnishings. The tabernacle declares that Israel is God's—God dwells with them. By carrying the tabernacle with them everywhere they go, the Israelites say to the rest of the world that God is among them and active.

In 1 Corinthians, Paul applies this image of God's dwelling place to believers. Paul writes, "Don't you know that you yourselves are God's temple and that God's Spirit dwells in your midst?" (1 Cor. 3:16). As God's presence dwelled in the tabernacle of ancient Israel, the Holy Spirit dwells in us today. We ourselves are God's way of declaring to the world that all people belong to God. We are to be telltale signs to the people around us that God is here and active, declaring to the whole world that Jesus is risen and he is King.

As we look forward to Jesus' death and resurrection, may we use this time of Lent to remember that each and every day of our lives declares Easter morning and says to the world, "God is here."

PRAYER

Take a few moments to reflect on Jesus' death and resurrection. How have they impacted your life? How has Jesus changed you?

God, you are majestic and glorious, Creator of the universe, yet you have chosen us as a means of showing yourself to the world. Help us to remove those things in our lives that point to ourselves, and fill us with those things that point to you. Amen.

CLOTHING

"These are the garments they are to make: a breastpiece, an ephod, a robe, a woven tunic, a turban and a sash. They are to make these sacred garments for your brother Aaron and his sons, so they may serve me as priests."

Read
Exodus 28:1-5

I love wearing a tuxedo. Give me an occasion to throw on the black coat, the vest, and the bowtie, and I relish it. The best part is the shoes. Those shoes shine with the reflected light of the room and click when I walk. They make me want to launch into a tap routine worthy of Fred Astaire (well, maybe not as good as him, but one can dream). The tuxedo announces that I am going somewhere special; I have a reason to dress up.

In Exodus 28, God gives Moses direction on the priestly garments that Aaron and the whole line of priests are to wear whenever they do their priestly work. In fact, the breastpiece, the ephod, the robe, the tunic, the turban, and the sash function as *the* priestly uniform; these are the garments that are needed *so that* Aaron and his family may serve as priests. This passage seems to imply that without the priestly clothing, Aaron isn't really a priest. When Aaron puts on the whole outfit, he announces to all people everywhere that he is going before God; he has a reason to dress up.

In Galatians 3:26-27, Paul writes, "So in Christ Jesus you are all children of God through faith, for all of you who were baptized into Christ have clothed yourselves with Christ." Becoming a Christian means that there is something distinct about us. We have put on different clothes, so to speak. Putting on the clothing of Jesus doesn't necessarily mean that we wear different physical clothing, but it does mean that something about us should announce to all people everywhere that we are going before God. We have a reason to dress up.

Colossians 3:12 says, "Therefore, as God's chosen people, holy and dearly loved, clothe yourselves with compassion, kindness, humility, gentleness, and patience." If these virtues are the tuxedo of the Christian life, then every day is a day to dress up.

PRAYER

Reflect for a few moments on what people see when they look at you. What "clothes" do they see? Do they see Jesus or do they see you?

God, help us to clothe ourselves with Jesus each and every day. Help us daily to put on compassion, kindness, humility, gentleness, and patience. Help us to show others that we have a reason to dress up. Amen.

HEROES

"I have given ability to all the skilled workers to make everything I have commanded you."

Read
Exodus 31:1-11

Our culture glorifies "lone ranger" superheroes. Peter Parker struggles to balance his everyday self and his superhero self, feeling overwhelmed by the task of saving the city again and again. But in the end, he's still Spiderman. The recent Batman movies remove any trace of Robin. Batman is alone, facing a task far bigger than he. We love the idea of the singular superhero, who, even when facing anxiety over the magnitude of the task, shoulders the burden and comes to the rescue of the world, typically getting the girl along the way.

In Exodus, we see a strikingly different picture of heroism.

As Moses nears the end of his time on the mountain, I wonder if he begins to feel some anxiety about the tasks God has given him. Throughout the chapters leading up to today's reading, God tells Moses again and again to build everything "as I have commanded you." Moses is given exact specifications about sizes, colors, and choice of metals and, so far, God has put the full responsibility on Moses. It's possible that Moses feels just a little overwhelmed.

In today's text, God calms Moses' anxieties. God tells Moses that the right people for the job have already been picked. God knows all of the skilled workers who will complete the tasks laid before Moses. It turns out that God has already set aside the right people for the job and given them the tools they need.

When we feel overwhelmed, we are often quick to take on a superhero mentality. We convince ourselves that we are the only ones who can finish our tasks; we are uniquely qualified for the work before us. We simply have to shoulder the burden and save the world.

Sometimes, we need to be reminded that we don't go through life alone. A true hero isn't the one who walks alone, but the one who recognizes that God has given others the skills that they need. Sometimes, a true hero is the person who reaches out for help, recognizing the limits of his or her own abilities and the giftedness of others.

Who might be the Bezalels and Oholiabs in *your* life?

PRAYER

What do you do when you are overwhelmed? Do you ever find it difficult to ask for help?

God, we are so often prideful people who think that it's all up to us. We often refuse to ask for help because we are afraid to admit our own weakness. Help us to recognize that you have blessed us with the body of believers to support us and encourage us, even when we are weak. Amen.

MUSIC

"For six days work is to be done, but the seventh day is a day of Sabbath rest, holy to the LORD."

Read Exodus 31:12-17

In 1952, crowds gathered at Woodstock, New York, to hear the latest piece by composer John Cage. Imagine the surprise of the audience when the pianist sat down, closed the piano lid, and sat still for thirty seconds. After opening the lid, he closed it once more, this time waiting two minutes and twenty-three seconds before opening the lid again. He closed the lid once more, this time for one minute and forty seconds. Thus the first performance of the piece called *4'33"* was complete.

While some may disagree with the definition of *4'33"* as "music," Cage was onto something. He realized that silence was not, in fact, silent. In order to hear and appreciate the music of the world around us, sometimes we need to silence the instruments.

In today's reading, God tells Moses to instruct the Israelites regarding the Sabbath day. It is to be a day of rest, a day when people do not work. This day is "holy to the Lord." God demands that the people of Israel live by a different calendar than those around them, recognizing a day set aside for God.

Many of us find it very difficult to take a regular Sabbath. The world around us tells us that we have work to do and there is no time for a break. Some of us are so busy volunteering on Sunday mornings that it hardly feels as though we have rested or worshipped at all. Sometimes the demands of conferences, school schedules, and last-minute projects simply get in the way of Sabbath rest.

Setting aside time for rest and worship does more than just give us a necessary day off. Sabbath rest creates a pattern that reserves time specifically for God. Sabbath demonstrates our trust that God will provide. Sabbath introduces a rhythm into our lives, a rhythm that helps open our hearts to the movement of the Holy Spirit. Six days, one day. Six days, one day.

Sometimes, to hear the voice of God, we need to silence the instruments.

PRAYER

What is the rhythm of your life? Is there time for rest and worship, for silence and breaks in the routine of your life? If not, how can you make room for Sabbath? If so, how balanced are the pauses with the busyness of everyday life?

God, we are a people who are constantly on the go. Our calendars are never further than our cell phones, our Facebook news feed clamors for our attention. Give us rest and give us pause so that we can hear your voice when the instruments are silent. Amen.

OSCAR

"Aaron took what they handed him and made it into an idol cast in the shape of a calf, fashioning it with a tool. Then they said, 'These are your gods, Israel, who brought you up out of Egypt.'"

Read
Exodus 32:1-6

Award shows like the Oscars are always fascinating. When it's time to give an acceptance speech, some people fall apart and forget themselves, often putting the network censors to the test. Some use the occasion to speechify or push a political agenda. But others receive their award with humility, remembering where they came from and who helped them get there.

In today's reading, the people of Israel have forgotten their history. They have forgotten that it was God who brought them out of Egypt. And they're sick of waiting for Moses. He's been gone a long time and it seems as if he won't be coming back. So they ask Moses' brother, Aaron, to make gods for them to worship.

And Aaron does. He collects all the gold jewelry from the people of Israel, melts it down, and forms a golden calf. We should pause here to ask a question: where did the Israelites get all that jewelry? They were, after all, slaves in Egypt. But in Exodus 12:36 we read, "The Lord made the Egyptians favorably disposed toward the people, and they gave them what they asked for; so they plundered the Egyptians." The very same jewelry that God allowed the people of Israel to collect from the Egyptians has been melted down to become the Israelites' idol.

The Israelites think their jewelry and all of the things that God caused the Egyptians to give them are the result of their own efforts and their own abilities. They decide to worship what they think are the fruits of their own labor.

We live and work in a culture that idolizes achievement. Some of us feel as if our worth depends on our total yearly sales. Or on our promotions. Or on the success of our children. Or on the number of research grants we secure for our institution.We begin to worship what we perceive as our own achievement.

When Moses is still on the mountain and it feels like we haven't heard from God in a while, do we forget our history? Do we forget who gave us the gold earrings?

PRAYER

Reflect for a few moments on the areas of your life where you have the most difficulty recognizing God as the source of your abilities.

God, you have blessed us in so many ways. You are the source of all our abilities, the Giver of every good and perfect gift. Help us to remember our history and to worship you, Creator and Sustainer of all, rather than ourselves. Amen.

GLOW

"When Moses came down from Mount Sinai with the two tablets of the covenant law in his hands, he was not aware that his face was radiant because he had spoken with the LORD."

Read Exodus 34:27-35

A few months ago I met a woman who was battling cancer. Every time she seemed to turn the corner, the cancer appeared again somewhere else. Her diagnosis kept getting worse and worse. Yet in spite of all her struggles, she couldn't help but smile as she shared her story. Her whole face glowed with peace and calm. Everyone around her felt the presence of God reflected in her.

When Moses comes down from Mount Sinai, his face is glowing with the radiance of God's presence. Everyone can see God reflected in Moses, who can't hide the encounter he has just had with the living God.

Most of us don't glow after we pray, after going to church, or after having devotions. Every so often we meet someone who is so overcome by joy that they glow—we normally see this glow at weddings, on the face of pregnant mothers, and at other moments of extraordinary joy. But we don't experience it firsthand on a regular basis.

Lent challenges us to spend time with God, to simply *be* in God's presence. We find it difficult to do so. After all, we have so many things on our "to do" lists. We have places to go and people to see and things that have to get done. But how often do we simply sit in silence, just be-ing before God?

Lent is a time of preparation, a time when we look ahead to Easter morning. Sunday mornings during Lent are a time of celebration, a foreshadowing of the joy of Easter. The story of Moses' radiant face reminds us of the infectious joy that we receive by spending time with God. When we allow ourselves to simply *be* with God, we find that the cares of the world melt away. Projects that we thought were important are put into perspective. Tasks that need to be finished still press upon us, but the burden of anxiety about them lightens. Our lives glow with the overflowing presence of the Holy Spirit, visible for all to see, inviting others to participate in the joy that comes from communion with our God.

PRAYER

Spend a few minutes in silence. Empty your mind. Don't think of what to say, simply be.

God, slow us down. Remind us to "be still and know that [you] are God." Give us the desire to cultivate the glow that comes from being with you, so that others can see you reflected in us. Amen.

FEAR

"Then Caleb . . . said, 'We should go up and take possession of the land, for we can certainly do it.' But the men who had gone up with him said, 'We can't attack those people; they are stronger than we are.'"

Read Numbers 13:25-31

The summer between my junior and senior years of high school, I attended a program for students interested in becoming pastors. I spent twenty-nine days learning about various kinds of ministry, visiting church plants in Calgary, Alberta, and getting to know other people who had dreams similar to my own.

For years I had told everybody I knew that I wanted to be a pastor. Within a few months my story was changing. I wasn't so sure anymore. I didn't know why I was beginning to doubt my chosen path, and it wasn't until years later that I realized the reason: I was afraid.

The time I spent in that summer program was amazing and I learned a lot. But I also saw myself next to some other people who were so much more qualified for the ministry than I was. I found myself thinking, "I'm not nearly as talented as Andrew." Or, "I don't have the excitement for preaching that Derek has." Or, "I'm not as compassionate as Erin." When I began to compare myself to those around me, I found my heart clouded by fear and my vision for God's direction in my life blurred.

Today's reading is a classic story of fear and anxiety taking over. The people of Israel have been promised that God will direct them and care for them as they move into the promised land, but they begin to compare themselves to their neighbors and fear gets in the way. In the past the people of Israel had a clear sense of where they were supposed to go and what they were supposed to do, but now they find themselves controlled by their anxiety.

It's easy for us to question why the Israelites would so quickly abandon God's direction. But I know from my own life how difficult it can be to trust God when I look at the situation around me and compare myself to others.

Thankfully, Paul assures us that following God's will isn't about our own talents and abilities: "But God said to me, 'My grace is sufficient for you, for my power is made perfect in weakness.' Therefore I will boast all the more gladly about my weaknesses, so that Christ's power may rest on me" (2 Cor. 12:9).

When fear and anxiety press upon us from all sides, may we cling to that promise.

PRAYER

Do you ever feel inadequate? Do you ever compare yourself to those around you?

God, we are quick to compare ourselves to our neighbors and put our trust in ourselves rather than in you. Help us to lean wholly on your name and to boast about our weaknesses, so that we may glorify the name of Jesus. Amen.

DESERT

> "As for your children that you said would be taken as plunder, I will bring them in to enjoy the land you have rejected."
>
> **Read** Numbers 14:26-35

In yesterday's reading I shared part of my calling story. Like the Israelites, I let fear and anxiety cloud my sense of where God might be calling me to go. I turned away from the direction that I had so clearly felt before.

My story, however, does not end there. Over the next few years, I pursued a degree in classical studies, including graduate work. I devoted all of my academic energies to studying the ancient world and its languages. But a year into my graduate work, I began to sense that God was calling me somewhere else. I finally recognized the fear that had kept me from the ministry and began my studies at seminary.

As I look at where I am today, I find it hard to imagine arriving here without my academic pursuits. God was able to take my fear and anxiety and use it to equip me for later work.

In today's story we find a foreshadowing glimpse of God's preparatory work. In the middle of a passage of judgment and punishment, God remains faithful: the children of the current generation will see the promised land. In fact, this generation will be shaped by their desert experience. During their wandering, they will be shepherds in the wilderness, and they must learn to depend on God.

As we look forward to Easter morning and to the resurrection of Jesus that overcomes sin and death, Lent is an opportunity to spend time in the desert. Lent is a time for our old selves to pass away and for our new life in Christ to flourish. Lent is a time for us to learn again to be God's people.

Perhaps spending time in the desert means setting aside time each week to spend with God, trusting that God will provide the time you need to finish your tasks. Perhaps it means going out of your way to serve those who are less fortunate. Perhaps it means opening up to somebody about that habit that you want to kick but can't on your own, asking them to hold you accountable.

What might your desert be?

PRAYER

Spend a few moments in quiet reflection. What are some of the deserts in your past that God has used to equip you for where you are today? How can you use Lent as a desert to prepare yourself for Easter morning?

God, you are the one who can turn even our failures to your glory. You are the one who is with us in the desert, who guides us through the wilderness and protects us through the storm. Bring us home rejoicing in the new life we have in Jesus. Amen.

BLESSING

"How beautiful are your tents, Jacob, your dwelling places, Israel!"

Read Numbers 23:27-24:9

In *Harry Potter and the Chamber of Secrets*, Harry visits the home of his best friend, Ron, for the first time. Ron's family does not have a lot of money and their house is not extravagant. Harry, however, has spent most of his childhood sleeping in a closet under the staircase. When they first arrive, Ron sheepishly tells Harry, "It's not much." Harry has the opposite reaction: "It's wonderful."

As Israel wanders the desert and moves closer to the Promised Land, they encounter various people groups who oppose their passage through the land. God protects the people of Israel in battle, and they are victorious again and again. The king of Moab hears of these battles and calls upon Balaam, an eastern prophet, to curse the people of Israel. While Balaam is traveling to Moab, he encounters an angel (and a talking donkey) who tells him to speak only what God says (see Numbers 22).

In our passage for today, Balaam has already blessed the people of Israel twice instead of cursing them. In his third blessing, Balaam looks upon the people of Israel for the first time. As he looks out over the people camped in the wilderness, the Spirit of God comes over him, and Balaam exclaims, "How beautiful are your tents, Jacob, your dwelling places, Israel!"

The people of Israel have been wandering in the desert. Their dwelling place is a place with no permanent home, little water, and scarce food. But when Balaam looks at them, he sees the people whom God delivered from Egypt, the people whom God has blessed and planted.

Sometimes, when we're facing tough times and find ourselves in the desert, it's easy to focus on current circumstances. We see only darkness and trouble. We are only able to see things from our own perspective.

It's important for us to actually turn and look at ourselves in the desert. Sometimes we need to be reminded of the ways in which God has guided us and protected us in the past and has blessed us and planted us where we are.

We may find ourselves saying, "How wonderful is my dwelling place!"

PRAYER

Reflect on some of the challenges in your life right now. Do you find yourself focusing on the difficulties and not on the ways God has blessed you in the past?

God, you have faithfully guided us and protected us through the storms of life. When we find ourselves overwhelmed by our circumstances, help us to turn our face toward the wilderness and see your hand at work in our lives. Amen.

REFUSAL

"'Let me go over and see the good land beyond the Jordan—that fine hill country and Lebanon.' . . . 'That is enough,' the LORD said, 'Do not speak to me anymore about this matter.'"

Read Deut. 3:21-29

In the movie *Yes Man*, Jim Carrey's character attends a presentation by a motivational speaker who convinces him that he should say yes to every opportunity that comes his way. At first, everything seems to be going great. He begins to succeed at work, meets a new love interest, and begins to experience life in new and exciting ways. Inevitably, however, his life begins to unravel as he approves too many dangerous bank loans, finds himself in dangerous circumstances, and is unable to take control of his life. Eventually, he learns that living a full and complete life is not the same as saying yes to everything.

We so often find ourselves wishing that God would always say yes. We feel that life would be so much easier if God would just give us what we want when we ask for it. We find ourselves impatiently waiting for God to give us the answer we want to our prayers.

"I'm sick of trying to make ends meet. I wish God would give me more stability at work."

"I'm tired of looking for direction. I don't know where God is leading me. I wish everything would be clearer."

In today's passage, Moses asks God one last time to be allowed to enter the Promised Land. God refuses Moses' request in a moment that might seem unfair to us. It seems a simple thing, to let Moses cross the river with the people. But Moses' request is more complicated than that. He doesn't just want to cross the Jordan River; he wants to explore, to visit the hill country and the coast. But the people of Israel are not yet done with their journey, and they need a leader who will guide them. God has already planned for Joshua to take over the leadership of Israel. God's refusal was not just a petty decision. God's plans were much bigger than anything Moses desired. God's refusal opens the way for the people of Israel.

Sometimes we wish that God would just say yes. We can trust, however, that God's refusal is not just a petty decision. God's refusal opens the way for something much bigger and better.

PRAYER

What prayers do you wish God would simply answer with a yes? How might God's refusal prepare you for something else?

God, we so often believe that we know what is best for ourselves and fail to put our trust in you. Help us to trust even your refusals. Amen.

WEDDINGS

> "These commandments that I give you today are to be on your hearts. Impress them on your children. Talk about them when you sit at home and when you walk along the road, when you lie down and when you get up."
>
> **Read**
> Deut. 6:1-9

When most couples get engaged, they are unable to talk about much else until the wedding day arrives. Dresses, flowers, invitations, registries, guest lists, and caterers dominate the conversation for weeks on end. Are we going to register for china or not? What pattern? Should we have a DJ or a live band?

In Deuteronomy 6, Moses encourages the people to have the same kind of enthusiasm for God's commandments as a couple about their upcoming wedding. These commandments are to be the central topic of conversation, around the dining room table, in the car, late into the night, and early in the morning. No moment of the Israelites' day is to go by without their excitement and passion for God's commands spilling over into a desire to share them with their families and their neighbors. No area of life is separated from this passionate love of God's commands.

For many of us, it is much easier to separate our faith from the rest of our lives than it is to integrate faith fully into our work and our recreation. We section off our lives so that our faith is for Sunday mornings and Monday through Saturday is something else entirely.

Deuteronomy 6 challenges us anew to break down the barriers between faith and learning, between faith and life, between faith and whatever else it is you want to put in that space.

Lent challenges us to reflect on the brokenness of the world revealed in our academic study, our work, and our relationships. Lent challenges us to see all redeeming elements of the world around us through the lens of Jesus' work on the cross. Lent challenges us to see every moment as an opportunity to tell others about the love of God.

At Lent, may the coming of Easter be so central in our hearts and our minds that, like a bride and groom waiting for their wedding day, it dominates all thought and conversation.

PRAYER

Spend a few moments basking in the joy of Easter's coming. Celebrate Jesus' lordship in all aspects of your life, including work, school, and family.

God, give us hearts that are filled with love of your Word. Help us to be so full of love for you that that love spills over into all aspects of our lives. Amen.

EXPECTATIONS

"As I was with Moses, so I will be with you; I will never leave you nor forsake you."

Read
Joshua 1:1-9

In 2006 and 2007, the University of Florida men's basketball team won back-to-back national championships. In both seasons, UF played with the same five players in the starting lineup. The 2008 team, with an all-new starting lineup, had big shoes to fill. Florida fans had come to expect excellence from their team and were disappointed by a season that couldn't meet the level of success of the past two years.

When Joshua takes over the leadership of Israel, he is stepping into a big role. Understandably, he seems to have a fair amount of anxiety over his new position. God encourages Joshua to be strong and courageous. Joshua does not need to fear the expectations that the people may have of him, for God promises, "I will never leave you nor forsake you."

Sometimes, we can feel overwhelmed by expectations. We put too much on our plate and feel the weight of multiple assignments, projects, and committees. We make too many promises to too many people and can't figure out how we'll get everything done. We look at the past and think we have to live up to the precedent set by those who have gone before us and feel that the bar is just too high.

When we begin to feel overwhelmed, God's promise to Joshua rings true once more for us today: "I will never leave you nor forsake you."

When the assignments are piling up and our research just won't come together, God says, "I will never leave you nor forsake you."

When the bills keep coming in and money seems to be tighter and tighter, God says, "I will never leave you nor forsake you."

No matter the circumstances, no matter how high the expectations, no matter how big the shoes we have to fill, God says, "I will never leave you nor forsake you."

PRAYER

What circumstances make you feel overwhelmed? How does God's promise speak to those circumstances?

God, you have promised that you will never leave nor forsake us. Help us to rest in that promise and to put our hope in you, even when the circumstances around us seem overwhelming. Amen.

STONES

> "In the future, when your children ask you, 'What do these stones mean?' tell them that the flow of the Jordan was cut off before the ark of the covenant of the LORD."
>
> **Read**
> Joshua 4:1-7

After forty years of wandering in the desert, Israel has finally crossed over the Jordan River into the Promised Land. The desert has prepared Israel to be God's people, a light to the Gentiles around them. Now, God causes the waters of the Jordan to dry up, allowing the Israelites to cross. The people step down into the river and come up to new life in God's Promised Land, leaving behind the desert. God's first command for the people in their new land: build a monument.

These twelve standing stones are a reminder to future generations of Israelites of what God did at the Jordan River that day. They remind the Israelites that their story is part of a much bigger story, that their family is much bigger than their own parents, village, or tribe. They remind future generations of Israelites that countless people have gone before them, all part of God's covenant family. When children ask, "What do these stones mean?" their parents tell them the story of God's people, the story in which they now participate.

On Easter morning, we encounter a new kind of standing stone. Lent looks forward to the stone rolled away from the grave on Easter morning, a stone that invites us to join in God's family. Around the world on Easter morning, countless people are gathered, pointing to the stone rolled away from the grave, reminded of God's covenant faithfulness. The stone rolled back tells us that the tomb is empty; Jesus has conquered sin and death so that we can have full life in him as part of God's covenant family. And when people all around the world point to the empty grave and ask, "What does this stone mean?" we can tell them the story of God's people, the story in which we now participate.

Standing stones remind us that we are part of something much bigger and grander than just our own personal salvation. They remind us that countless people have gone down into the Jordan and come up into new life in the Promised Land. They remind us that we are part of God's story for the whole world, a story that affects all areas of life.

The stone sits beside the empty tomb and everyone wants to know, "What does this stone mean?" How will we answer?

PRAYER

Reflect on the majesty and greatness of Easter and the scope of salvation. How do we participate in God's story today?

God, the stone has been rolled back and the grave is empty. Fill us with joy and awe at the majesty of that day and the glory of Jesus. Help us to feel a part of your covenant family this day. Amen.

CONSEQUENCES

"So they divided the land they were to cover, Ahab going in one direction and Obadiah in another."

Read
1 Kings 18:1-8

The law of unintended consequences states that for every purposeful action in a complex system, one can expect unforeseen consequences. Some of these consequences might be good, others bad. For example, ships sunk during wartime have now become coral reefs, a positive unintended consequence; rent control in large cities, intended to keep costs low, can create housing shortages. In other words, the complexity of our interaction with the world makes it impossible for us to be fully aware of every consequence of our actions.

In 1 Kings 18, Ahab experiences this to some degree. Facing a famine and a drought, Ahab decides to send Obadiah one direction in search of water while he goes another direction. Obadiah, a faithful servant of God, runs into Elijah, who is on his way to Ahab. When we consider the details, we realize that this is no chance encounter. If God had told Elijah to go earlier, Obadiah would not have been out searching. If Ahab and Obadiah had gone in opposite directions, Elijah would have met Ahab instead of Obadiah. God providentially arranged this encounter between Elijah and Obadiah.

One of the profoundly wondrous things about God is this: God is not subject to the law of unintended consequences.

God is bigger than the most complex system. God fully understands every consequence of every decision in ways that we cannot, and so we can trust that God will provide whatever we need for body and soul. God sees every action that takes place within the complex systems of the world, and we can trust that God will turn to good whatever adversity comes to us in this sad world.

As we explore the story of Elijah together this week, let us rejoice that we worship a God who is bigger than the law of unintended consequences.

PRAYER

Consider a time where your actions had unintended consequences. Consider your personal limitations that caused these consequences. Now reflect on the greatness of God, who is not subject to such limitations.

God, sometimes it can be difficult for us to trust that you hold all things in your hands. Help us to rest in your providence, trusting that you understand the consequences of every action. Amen.

SALAD

"So Obadiah went to meet Ahab and told him, and Ahab went to meet Elijah."

Read
1 Kings 18:8-16

Until recently, I hated salads. Lettuce made me gag, and drowning it in dressing didn't make it any better. Two years ago, I gave up eating meat (including fish) for Lent. I quickly realized that I needed to add salads as a regular part of my diet if I wished to find food I could eat. Grudgingly, I tried a new salad place that had just opened down the street and, lo and behold, I loved it. My own anxiety had gotten in the way of experiencing something delicious.

In today's passage, Elijah commands Obadiah to announce his presence to Ahab. Obadiah protests, arguing that doing so will put his life at risk. He doubts whether Elijah will keep his word and show up as promised. Obadiah hesitates to follow Elijah's command because of fear and anxiety.

Obadiah does not meet an untimely end. His fears were groundless. In fact, the narrative sequence is simple and straightforward—Obadiah tells Ahab, and Ahab leaves to meet Elijah. Obadiah's fears and assumptions about Elijah nearly prevent Obadiah from experiencing God's work on Mt. Carmel. His job was simply to follow Elijah's call.

We often let fear dominate our decision-making. We feel called to follow God's will in our lives but let anxiety get in the way.

"I want to tell my coworkers that I'm a Christian, but I worry about offending someone or losing my job."

"I feel called to enroll in this graduate program, but the financial package seems much better at this other university. Shouldn't I just follow the money?"

Notice that Elijah does not promise Obadiah that everything will be OK. Instead, he simply promises, "I will surely present myself to Ahab today." The point of the story is not that Ahab doesn't kill Obadiah, but that Obadiah obeys despite his anxiety.

God does not promise us that life is going to be easy or everything will be perfect. Choosing to follow God's will instead of giving in to our fear and anxiety is not a recipe for instant success. It is not a recipe for health and wealth. We can trust, however, that we will find God's presence when we stand up for what is right.

And life in God's presence is where we're meant to be.

PRAYER

What anxiety do you have about following God in your own life?

God, calm our fear and anxiety. When we hesitate to follow you, give us strength and courage. Help us to experience your presence and full life. Amen.

MULTITASK

"Elijah went before the people and said, 'How long will you waver between two opinions? If the LORD is God, follow him; but if Baal is God, follow him.'"

Read
1 Kings 18:20-29

I recently watched a CNBC special on smartphones. One of the things that interested me most was the ability of cell phone users to multitask and pay attention to multiple things that are happening. In one example, researchers asked a college student to send a text message while walking across campus. While the student focuses on sending the text, a clown approaches from the opposite direction, juggling and riding a unicycle. The student, oblivious, walks right past. Despite claiming to be a talented multitasker, the student denied noticing anything unusual while sending the message. Cell phones compete for our attention and draw our focus.

In today's passage, Elijah calls upon the people of Israel to stop trying to multitask with their religious affections. The people should follow the God who is truly God and deserving of their allegiance. Elijah then watches as the prophets of Baal unsuccessfully try to call upon their god. The prophets of Baal try harder, devoting themselves entirely to Baal. But in the end, it's worthless: "There was no response, no one answered, no one paid attention."

Most of us will not be presented with a choice between worshipping Baal and worshipping God. However, we do encounter things every day that compete for our love and attention. What will get ahold of our heart? Our jobs, our successes, our money, our fame, our talent, our friends—all of these seek our affection in and of themselves.

Every day, we choose whom and how we will love. Will we love our job or will we love God with our job? Will we love our family or will we love God with our family?

Every day, Elijah's voice calls back to us from Mt. Carmel: "If the LORD is God, follow him."

PRAYER:

What things do you love most of all? How can you love these things in such a way that they help you love God more?

God, you are the desire of our hearts. Help us to love you with all of our heart, all of our soul, all of our mind, and all of our strength. Amen.

FIRE

"Answer me, LORD, answer me, so these people will know that you, LORD, are God, and that you are turning their hearts back again."

Read
1 Kings 18:30-38

Any good science experiment must be replicable. That is, in order to trust the results of a scientific study, the researchers must explain the process by which they arrived at their results so that others can recreate the same experiment and validate the original findings. This process is an integral part of the scientific method.

When I read today's story, I find myself wishing that I were able to replicate the scene on Mt. Carmel. It seems like it would be a lot easier to share the gospel if I could call down fire from heaven in order to demonstrate God's power to those around me. I have sometimes wondered why I can't do this if Elijah could. What if I gathered a group of people and prayed for God to perform a miraculous sign in order that they would believe. Why would God most likely not answer that prayer?

On the one hand, I know the "right" theological answers. I know that we are called to have faith and to put our trust in things unseen. I know that Jesus told Thomas, "Blessed are those who have not seen and yet have believed" (John 20:29). But sometimes, I wonder, "Is it really so bad to be a Thomas?" If Elijah could ask God to put on a miraculous display of power, why can't we?

There is something very natural about these questions. I don't think there's anything wrong with asking them, and we can ask them from a variety of motives ranging from a desire to have our faith confirmed to an honest desire for others to see God.

But when I look around the world, I find God putting on miraculous displays all around us if we just have eyes to see.

God's majesty is in the complex structure of a grain protein and the intricacy of a baby's ear.

God's beauty is in the soaring melody of classical music and the rustle of the leaves in a cool fall breeze.

God's glory is found in the shifting tides of markets and the weight of ancient tragedy.

Everywhere we look, God rains down fire from heaven so that all may see, if only we keep our eyes open.

PRAYER

Where do you encounter God in your own life?

God, give us eyes to see you as we encounter your world. Give us ears to hear you as you speak to us in love. Give us hands to do your work as we interact with one another. Give us feet to go wherever you may send us. Amen.

RUNNING

"The power of the LORD came on Elijah and, tucking his cloak into his belt, he ran ahead of Ahab all the way to Jezreel."

Read
1 Kings 18:39-46

I have a lot of respect for runners. I see them in their spandex, running through rain and snow, jogging alongside the road, and I think to myself, "How do you do that?!" I know that running is good for you, but I just can't stand it. Ask me if I want to go running, and I will politely decline. Or I might tell you that I hate running. Either way, I won't go.

In today's passage, the power of the Lord comes on Elijah, and he decides to go for a seventeen-mile run down the mountain. Seventeen miles to the home of King Ahab. Seventeen miles to Ahab's murderous wife, Jezebel, who also wants Elijah dead. Seventeen miles after exhaustion has already overtaken him at the top of Mt. Carmel. Seventeen miles from danger into danger. Seventeen miles only by the power of God.

Some days, we feel as though we have spent every last amount of energy we have in reserve. Some days, we feel so exhausted from work, school, and other responsibilities that we simply do not know where we will possibly find the energy to do anything else that day. Some days, we feel overwhelmed, overworked, and overstressed. And some days, we feel as though we go from one situation to another, constantly on the alert and constantly watching our backs. Some days, we wonder where we will find the strength.

We can trust, however, that God will give us the strength to carry on. Maybe you're not called to run seventeen miles in the rain (I hope I'm not). But in those weeks when the tasks keep coming at us and there is simply no end in sight, we fix our eyes on Jesus, tuck our cloak into our belt, and run, putting our trust in God for our strength.

PRAYER

What do you need strength to complete today?

God, you have said to us, "Come to me, all who are weary and heavy laden, and I will give you rest." We are in need of your rest today. Give us your strength and give us your peace as we seek to run the race set out before us. Amen.

LOW

"So he got up and ate and drank. Strengthened by that food, he traveled forty days and forty nights until he reached Horeb, the mountain of God."

Read
1 Kings 19:1-9a

During Lent, we have focused our attention on various biblical narratives of "forty"—Noah in the ark for forty days, Moses on Mount Sinai for forty days, the Israelites in the desert for forty years. Today we encounter Elijah traveling for forty days and forty nights to Mount Horeb.

I find the placement of today's story within the framework of this narrative interesting. At the beginning of chapter 18, the word of the Lord comes to Elijah; he encounters Obadiah; he presents himself to Ahab; he displays the power of God on Mt. Carmel. Then today, he runs in fear from Ahab, becomes overwhelmed with depression, and spends forty days traveling. Elijah seemingly has every reason to be at a spiritual high—I imagine many of us would feel especially close to God if we had just called down fire from heaven. Instead, Elijah finds himself at his most vulnerable.

In the course of our spiritual journeys, we encounter a range of highs and lows. There are days when we feel incredibly close to God and days when we feel completely alone. There are days where we feel like we are walking in step with God, only to receive a phone call with bad news from a loved one. Sometimes, the moments of closeness to God are followed immediately by days of pain, sorrow, and confusion.

God's response to Elijah was not to immediately make everything better. Instead, God sends Elijah just enough to sustain him and sends him into the wilderness, back to Mt. Horeb. Elijah spends forty days walking with his questions. Forty days with his pain. Forty days feeling as though he has failed. Forty days wondering what happened.

When we enter the low periods of our spiritual journey, those moments when we wonder where God is, we want God to respond immediately. But sometimes, God gives us just enough to sustain us, and then asks us to wait for a while. Sometimes, God asks us to spend time with our questions, to spend time with our pain, to spend time wondering what has happened.

That's what Lent is all about.

PRAYER

Where are you in your spiritual life? Are you between Mt. Carmel and Mt. Horeb, like Elijah in today's story? What might God teach you in this place between the mountains?

God, you are the one who nourishes and sustains us. Help us to see the ways in which low periods of our spiritual lives may actually be preparation for something much greater. Amen.

WHISPER

"After the earthquake came a fire, but the LORD was not in the fire. And after the fire came a gentle whisper."

Read
1 Kings 19:9b-18

Forty days of traveling has brought Elijah to Mt. Horeb. As he waits to encounter God's presence, the mountain is first rocked by a powerful wind, then an earthquake, and finally a fire. But these powerful acts of nature do not reveal God. God is revealed after the fire in a gentle whisper.

On Easter Sunday, Jesus rose from the grave, conquering sin and death. Jesus demonstrated on Easter Sunday that God's love is more powerful than all of the forces of evil—God's power has triumphed. A new world order has come and Jesus is Lord over all creation. The royal proclamation does not go out, however, with the voice of a trumpet or with flame coming down from heaven.

The good news of Easter morning is proclaimed in the gentle voices of the women at the tomb, who go forth to tell the disciples.

The women tell the disciples, the disciples tell each other, and one by one word begins to spread: "He is risen!" The new order of creation, the eternal lordship of Jesus

Christ, is present in the gentle voice of God's people sharing the good news with everyone they meet.

We are always tempted to fall back on showy displays of God's power. We want to call down fire from heaven. We can think that our testimony isn't exciting enough, our lives aren't good enough, our faith isn't strong enough to share the gospel. We think that we are not gifted in evangelism or that it's not our job.

But the voice of God comes to Elijah in a gentle whisper. The proclamation of Easter morning goes out through the voices of the women. The good news of Jesus goes out every day in the voices of God's people, one gentle voice at a time.

Will you tell the story?

PRAYER

What keeps you from telling the story of Easter?

God, help us to overcome our fears and anxieties. Give us the words to share your gospel and to tell others the good news. Help us say to everyone we meet, in word and in deed, "He is risen." Amen.

BUT . . . (PART 1)

"But Jonah ran away from the LORD and headed for Tarshish."

Read
Jonah 1:1-5

When you really know somebody well, you can tell when they're trying to hide a "but." If you ask their opinion on a paint color, an outfit, or an idea, you know there's something unfinished about their response. There's more to it that they want to say; you're just not sure what it is. You know there's a "but."

Jonah is one of the more well-known examples of this in the Bible. God tells Jonah to go preach in Nineveh, *but* Jonah runs away. Plain and simple, Jonah disobeys. Jonah knows what he is supposed to do but simply does not want to do it.

I think it is easy for most of us to relate to Jonah. We might not be called to preach destruction on a great city, but we certainly encounter opportunities where the right choice is blatantly obvious but we make the wrong one anyway.

We overlook the opportunity to help somebody in need.

We fudge the numbers on our taxes.

We click that link on the internet.

We act like everyone else around us.
We go to Tarshish when God calls us to Nineveh.
Where are you going?

PRAYER

Can you remember a time when you were going to Tarshish instead of Nineveh?

God, help us to see the ways to honor and glorify your name and then to act on them. Grant us your forgiveness for those times when we choose to go our own way instead of yours. Amen.

IDENTITY

"[Jonah] answered, 'I am a Hebrew and I worship the LORD, the God of heaven, who made the sea and the dry land.'"

Read
Jonah 1:5-16

I recently read a book called *Damaged Identities* by a philosopher from Michigan State University. The author, Hilde Lindemann Nelson, explores the ways in which we and those around us construct our identities. To some extent, we get to create our own identity—we tell the story of who we are and what matters most to us. At the same time, those we interact with also have a role to play in creating our identity—they can accept or reject the stories we tell about ourselves or can tell their own stories about who we are. In other words, part of our identity is based on the way others react to and interact with us.

In today's text, Jonah is asked to give an account of his own identity and to tell his story. Jonah responds by identifying himself primarily by his religious practice. Jonah describes God as the one "who made the sea and the dry land" and is thus able to save the sailors from their current predicament. The sailors, however, demonstrate by their actions that they don't buy Jonah's story. They try to get out of the storm and attempt to row for land, even after

Jonah asks to be thrown into the water to stop the storm. Jonah identifies himself by his worship of the Lord, but the sailors see a contradiction in his actions and construct a different identity for Jonah.

If you identify yourself as a "Christian," a "Christ-follower," a "Jesus freak," or anything else that demonstrates your commitment to Jesus Christ, people around you will evaluate the story you tell of your identity. When we act in ways that are not in harmony with the identity we have shared, those around us may question whether that narrative is really true. When this happens, people see a contradiction in our actions and construct a different identity for us.

We know the words they use: "Hypocrite." "Liar." "Holier-than-thou."

What story do the actions of your life tell? When others look at you, do they see the same person you claim to be?

PRAYER

What actions in your life may not be consistent with your faith? How do others respond to these actions?

God, help us to see those things in our lives that do not align with our identity as people born again by your Spirit. Amen.

BUT . . . (PART 2)

"To the roots of the mountains I sank down; the earth beneath barred me in forever. But you, LORD my God, brought my life up from the pit."

Read
Jonah 1:17-2:10

One day I was trying to figure out how to connect my laptop to the network at my office. I'm fairly adept technologically, so I figured I could do it on my own. When I unplugged the network cable from my desktop computer, tugged on it for some slack, and plugged it in to my laptop, I was surprised to find that it didn't work. I followed the cable to a compartment blocked off by a wood panel. Still relying on my own technological know-how, I removed the wood panel and began examining the network router inside. Much to my dismay, my tugging and pulling had broken the main cable to the router, knocking out the network in half of the church. Sheepishly, I went to the main office, finally asking to be rescued from the situation into which I had put myself.

In today's passage, Jonah has literally and figuratively been brought to the depths. On Monday, we encountered Jonah's "but"—God commands, *but* Jonah goes his own way. Today, we encounter God's "but"—Jonah finds himself sinking into the depths of his own sin, *but* God brings his life up from the pit.

When we think about the people we encounter every day, we see signs of brokenness all around us. Marriages fall apart, friendships turn sour, and every day myriad people seek solace in the bottom of a bottle or the embrace of meaningless sex.

We find, time and time again, that we run from God, seeking to do our own thing and trying to go down our own path. The story of our lives is filled with our "buts."

The message of the gospel is God's "but."

We were lost in sin, but Jesus died on the cross.

We were spiritually dead, but God poured out the Holy Spirit on us.

We were sinking in our own brokenness, but God brought our life up from the pit.

And our response to that can only be to say with Jonah, "Salvation comes from the LORD."

PRAYER

Have you ever been in a situation where you needed someone to rescue you? What was that like?

God, when we are in the depths we cry to you, and you answer us. Thank you for pouring out your Spirit on us so we may have new life. Amen.

PIE

"Jonah began by going a day's journey into the city, proclaiming, 'Forty more days and Nineveh will be overthrown.'"

Read
Jonah 3:1-5

A couple of days ago I went for a slice of pie from a local restaurant. I love their crumb crust pies. The problem is, whenever you make or buy an entire pie, you have to slice it. If I slice a pie, inevitably a few slices will be smaller than others. I noticed that this restaurant has the perfect solution: a pie slicer that divides the pie into six equal-sized pieces. No worries about getting the smallest slice! No worries about whether one child received a bigger piece than another. Each slice is a perfect one-sixth of the pie.

In today's passage, Jonah finally obeys God and preaches to the city of Nineveh. Surprisingly, however, we discover that Jonah only covers one-third of the ground of the city. He begins with this first third, but this is the last we hear of Jonah's preaching. It's as though Jonah agrees to follow God's command, but then does the minimum necessary to feel as though he has obeyed. If God asked Jonah for a slice of pie, Jonah would give the smallest slice. Jonah obeys, but only half-heartedly (or *third*-heartedly!).

Sometimes, we obey God, but only with a third of our hearts. We do God's will, but only to the minimum extent possible. God invites us to give of our hearts and our lives, but we hold back.

We give our hearts to God, as long as God doesn't touch our work or studies.

We give our hearts to God, as long as God leaves our finances alone.

We give our hearts to God, as long as God blesses our efforts.

We give our hearts to God, as long as God is content with a third of it. Or a fourth. Or less.

Like Jonah, we go a third of the way into the city and stop. We give God the smallest slice of pie, when God asked for the whole pie.

What do you hold back from God?

PRAYER

Reflect on those areas of your life that you have the most difficulty giving to God. Consider especially your finances, your relationships, and your work. How can you give these to God?

God, you have commanded us to offer our whole hearts to you. We are so often content with giving you only a fraction of our life. Help us to find those areas that we hold back and offer them freely to you. Amen.

GREEN

"This is the proclamation [the king] issued in Nineveh: 'By the decree of the king and his nobles: Do not let people or animals, herds or flocks, taste anything; do not let them eat or drink.'"

Read
Jonah 3:6-10

Natural disasters have a tendency to dominate news headlines. Japan continues to recover from the tsunami. New Orleans is still recovering from the disaster of Hurricane Katrina. Haiti is still in disrepair from the 2010 earthquake. It doesn't take us long to realize that the created world suffers along with us from the effects of sin and destruction.

In today's reading, the king of Nineveh issues a decree commanding repentance from all people and all *animals*. Even the flocks and herds are to participate in this citywide act of repentance by wearing sackcloth and participating in a fast from food and drink. Everybody and everything is to live and act in recognition of God.

The last few years have seen the rise of the green movement, encouraging people everywhere to live sustainably. I am always amazed by the number of times I hear people within the church resist such environmental efforts. The church has often been guilty of having an attitude of "preside, populate, and pave" rather than one that seeks to sustain and nourish God's creation.

Most of us don't own large flocks and wouldn't dream of forcing our pets to fast from food and water. We can, however, help the created world fast in other ways.

We can choose to carpool.

We can recycle.

We can heat our homes efficiently.

We can turn the air conditioning a degree or two warmer.

We can buy more efficient light bulbs.

The list goes on and on. Being green isn't about saving money. It's not about reducing our dependency on foreign oil. It's not even about saving the planet. Certainly all of these are important.

It's about proclaiming a fast for everyone and everything as all of creation worships God.

PRAYER

How do you respond to green initiatives? How can you help the created world fast in your own life?

God, we see signs all around us of how creation cries out to you. Show us the ways in which we can help your creation proclaim you more fully. Amen.

MOTIVE

"Isn't this what I said, LORD, when I was still at home? That is what I tried to forestall by fleeing to Tarshish."

Read
Jonah 4:1-4

Crime dramas regularly use motive as a means to tug at the heartstrings of their audiences. A serial killer receives no pity from anyone in the show. A spouse who kills after learning of an affair is understood to be rightly angry, even though their action was wrong. The ones that get you, though, are the cases of mistaken identity. Somebody thought they were protecting their loved ones but accidentally killed one of them instead. As the story reveals the details of the killer's motive, the audience changes its attitude towards the crime.

Today, we finally discover Jonah's motive for running away to Tarshish. Many of us hear the story of Jonah and assume that he ran away because he was afraid. We might think that the idea of preaching a message of condemnation in such a powerful city scared Jonah.

But then we learn Jonah's true motive. He didn't want God to forgive the people of Nineveh. He tried to run away to keep God from showing compassion to the people he hated. He is so angry that God would do this that he wants to die. We learn his motive and our opinion of him changes. He's petty, self-centered, and stingy with God's love. He only wants the "right sort" of people to experience it.

And then we realize that we're the same as Jonah.

As much as we may know that the message of the gospel is for everyone, part of us wants to hold onto it for ourselves. As much as we know that Jesus reaches out to the sinners and outcasts of society, we don't want them in our churches.

Many of us don't want strippers, drug addicts, ex-convicts, and social outcasts in our church. We want to keep them an arm's length away. We can be petty, self-centered, and stingy with God's love. We only want the "right" kind of people.

Until we realize what God has done for us, that we are no better, that we all need Jesus.

At the cross we find God, who is gracious and compassionate, slow to anger and abounding in love. And God invites all of us to join the family.

PRAYER

Who do you encounter who needs to experience the love of God? What holds you back from offering it to them?

God, show us the people who need to experience your love. Help us to reach out with arms of compassion. Help us to show them your graciousness and abounding love. Amen.

CONCERN

"And should I not have concern for the great city of Nineveh, in which there are more than a hundred twenty thousand people who cannot tell their right hand from their left—and also many animals?"

Read
Jonah 4:5-11

If I were to write a story, I would probably not end it the way that the book of Jonah ends. At first glance, it seems to end with an anticlimactic *thud* rather than any sort of bang. The book of Jonah ends with this question from God: "Should I not have concern for Nineveh?" We are left scratching our heads, wondering what kind of an ending that is.

In order to understand this question, we need to think about who and what Nineveh represents to the people of Israel. Nineveh is the capital city of Assyria and the center of everything that Israel dislikes. The people of Israel constantly feel under threat from the people of Assyria. They are the kingdom who might sweep in at any moment and destroy their nation. They are the nation who destroys entire people groups, and they're also a hotbed of injustice.

And so this is a tough question: "Should I not have concern for Nineveh?" Maybe the question today would be, "Should I not have concern for radical extremists?"

We have Ninevehs in our personal lives too. People who represent everything we dislike. People who seem to go out of their way to make life difficult for us. And the question is the same: "Should I not have concern for even these?"

The question reveals how wide and expansive God's love is. God's love is bigger than terrorist networks. God's love is bigger than oppressive dictators. God's love is bigger than the colleague we don't get along with or the high school friendship turned sour.

The whole book of Jonah has been leading to this. God cares for Nineveh, and so should Jonah.

And so God poses the question to us again today, "Should I not have concern for Nineveh?"

PRAYER

Reflect for a few minutes on the people you find it difficult to love, both in your own life and on a more global scale. How can you show love to them?

God, your love and compassion are not bounded by national differences or by office politics. Help us to show love to each and every person we meet, especially those with whom we do not get along. Amen.

FLESH

"After fasting forty days and forty nights, he was hungry."

Read
Matthew 4:1-11

For the past four weeks, we have explored the biblical motif of forty—Noah on the ark for forty days; Moses on the mountain for forty days; Israel in the desert for forty years; Elijah on the run for forty days; and Jonah announcing forty days until impending destruction for the people of Nineveh. In all of these narratives, we have found foreshadowing of the gospel—reminders of Easter morning in light of what has come before.

In these last two weeks of Lent, we turn at last to Jesus. We meet the one for whom every forty-day period of preparation has been waiting. In Jesus we find the answer to Noah's rainbow, the living Word of Moses, the true deliverance for God's people from their desert wanderings, the voice of God walking the earth, the salvation for all people of every nation.

And in today's reading, we find Jesus in the desert. We meet Jesus after forty days of fasting, and he's hungry.

Like you and me, Jesus, the culmination of the whole biblical narrative, is hungry. He's vulnerable. He's human.

In the last two weeks of Lent, we will encounter Jesus as he experiences unimaginable suffering and very real emotions.

The gospel of John says, “The Word became flesh.” The Christian church calls it the incarnation. For our sake, in order to save all of humanity and all of creation, the eternal Son of God became a human being.

Let us use these last two weeks to recapture the wonder and amazement of the incarnation.

PRAYER

Do you tend to focus on Jesus as the Son of God or as truly human? How does the incarnation amaze you?

God, as we have met you over the last few weeks in the stories of your people, help us to meet you now again in the person of Jesus. Help us to recapture our amazement and wonder at the God who becomes one of us. Amen.

TAXES

"While Jesus was having dinner at Matthew's house, many tax collectors and sinners came and ate with him and his disciples."

Read
Matthew 9:9-13

Lent typically falls near the due date for federal income taxes. If you haven't filed yet, you might want to do that soon. If you use TurboTax, you'll be given the option to purchase Audit Defense, just in case the IRS comes knocking to follow up on any of your numbers.

In Jesus' day, the tax collectors were more than just IRS or CRA agents who might come and audit your numbers.

They were traitors.

The Romans knew how to manage an empire, and one way they did so was to put locals in charge of collecting local taxes. The Roman officials turned a blind eye when the tax collectors would charge a little extra on top for themselves. Tax collectors sold out to the oppressive Roman rule so they could watch out for their own livelihood.

They were despised.

And yet, here in Matthew 9, Jesus calls Matthew to be his disciple and joins a table of tax collectors and sinners for dinner with the rest of his disciples. Imagine the scandalized look on the face of anyone who might have seen them.

This meal is about more than reaching out to the outcasts of society. This meal brings together people from every walk of life at one table in a meal that transcends political sympathies. What matters most is Matthew's decision to follow Jesus.

When we faithfully follow Jesus, we will find ourselves in the company of people different from ourselves. We may find ourselves next to an ex-convict, a recovering alcoholic, a drug addict, a member of the opposing political party, or someone from a different ethnic background.

And we find that the only thing that matters is Jesus' invitation: "Follow me."

PRAYER

What groups of people do you feel uncomfortable around? Reflect for a few minutes on the reasons for your attitude and how you can show the love of Jesus to these people.

God, you bring together young and old, left and right, rich and poor. You gather your people from every walk of life and from every corner of the earth. As we join at your banquet table, help us to break down the barriers between us and enjoy your lavish feast together. Amen.

EXPECTATIONS

"'Where did this man get this wisdom and these miraculous powers?' they asked. 'Isn't this the carpenter's son?'"

Read Matthew 13:53-58

I attended the same high school that my parents did. One day while I was a freshman, a teacher whom I had never met before walked past me in the hallway. He took one look at me, smiled, and said, "You must be Chuck's son."

Hometowns and areas with which we are familiar have a tendency to breed expectations. Attending the same school as parents and siblings can result in unexpected recognition by people we have never met. When we walk into the store, we are bound to bump into somebody we know, even if years have gone by. People expect us to act like our parents, our siblings, or the people we were when they used to know us.

When Jesus returns to his hometown, his former neighbors and peers find themselves confused by the person who has come to town. They know Joseph and Mary. They know James, Joseph, Simon, and Judas. They know Jesus' sisters.

And Jesus is nothing like them.

When Jesus teaches, there is something different. When Jesus speaks, he is more than a man. He is more than Mary's son or James's brother.

Sometimes, we bring our own expectations of who Jesus is or should be. We think that Jesus should be a magic talisman who will make us healthy and wealthy. We think that Jesus should make everything go perfectly for us. We think that Jesus should give us what we want every time we want it. We want Jesus to be our friend but not our Lord.

During Lent, we encounter the person of Jesus, whose life and teaching transform our heart. We meet the Jesus who breaks through our outer defenses and speaks to the core of our being. We discover that Jesus is the source of all wisdom.

The question is this: how will we respond? Will we, like the people of Jesus' hometown, take offense at this man who is so much more than a man?

Or will we give our lives to him?

PRAYER

What expectations do you have of Jesus? How does Jesus defy these?

God, we each bring our own expectations for what you should do for us. We get frustrated when things don't go our way. Help us to feel the voice of Jesus speaking to our heart today. Amen.

FACEBOOK

"Simon Peter answered, 'You are the Messiah, the Son of the living God.'"

Read Matthew 16:13-20

The *LA Times* recently published an article about how our Facebook habits demonstrate something about our own sense of self-worth. We post pictures of ourselves to create a desired appearance. We use photos of ourselves in large groups to demonstrate that we belong, to say, "Look how popular I am!" Facebook and other social networking sites are tools we use to build our identity.

In today's passage, Jesus asks his disciples a natural question: "Who do people say the Son of Man is?" The disciples' report is telling—John the Baptist, Elijah, Jeremiah, and the other prophets were passionate people on fire for God. But these answers miss something. These comparisons don't address the true answer to Jesus' question.

So he asks his disciples, "Who do you say I am?"

Peter's declaration stands in sharp contrast to popular opinions about Jesus. Everyone else has made human comparisons. But Peter declares that Jesus is the Messiah—the long-awaited savior of Israel. He recognizes that Jesus is distinctly *unlike* those who have come before.

When people look at Jesus' life, they have many responses. Many people believe that Jesus was simply a "great teacher," others that he was completely crazy. Many are not sure that Jesus ever existed. And there are plenty of people who believe Jesus was a good guy whose later followers made up stories to justify their belief that he was more than human.

The church is not immune from this. Some want Jesus to be a pacifist; others want him to be a patriot. Some want him to herald their cause; others use him to oppress. Some want Jesus to be the emotional experience of a moving worship service; others want him to be a dogmatic set of beliefs and theological premises.

But Jesus is more than all that.

He is the Messiah, the Son of the living God.

Jesus turns to us today with the same question: "But what about you? Who do you say I am?"

PRAYER

Who is Jesus to you? What box do you try to put Jesus into? How does Jesus break out of that box?

Jesus, help us to recognize that you are more than the limitations we put on you. Help us to recognize that you are more than our theological premises, more than our friend, our cause, or our political backer. Help us to recognize you as our Messiah and our God. Amen.

TRANSFIGURED

"While he was still speaking, a bright cloud covered them, and a voice from the cloud said, 'This is my Son, whom I love; with him I am well pleased. Listen to him!'"

Read
Matthew 17:1-9

At the end of Disney's *Beauty and the Beast,* the Beast, apparently dead, is raised into the air and begins to glow. Light shines from each of his limbs as he is transformed from the Beast into a handsome prince. Belle's love has brought forth the true identity of the prince within.

The account of the transfiguration is one of those biblical passages that we often don't know what to do with. The details seem like they come out of a fairy tale—Elijah and Moses appear; Jesus begins to glow; there's a cloud and a voice. Jesus tells the disciples not to talk about it—we don't talk about it much either.

In Matthew 16, Peter confesses that Jesus is the Messiah. Immediately after this, Jesus begins to predict his own death. In chapter 17, Jesus begins to travel to Jerusalem. The story of the transfiguration is Jesus' first step toward Jerusalem, the first step toward his coming death. At this point, the cloud appears and the voice of the Father confirms the identity of the Son. The transfiguration reveals the true identity of Jesus as the Son of God.

This event was meant to be one by which the disciples would prove the identity of Jesus. Jesus asks the disciples to keep it a secret until he has been raised from the dead—implying that afterward, they are free to share the story. They would go forth and announce to all that the voice of God commanded them to listen to Jesus, God's Son.

Like the disciples, we too are called to go forth and share the story of Jesus, the Son of God. Like the disciples, we too share the story of how we have seen Jesus' true identity. We may not see Jesus transfigured, but we see lives transformed by the grace of God. We experience the forgiveness of our sins and the reconciliation with our brothers and sisters. Like the disciples, we recognize that Jesus has been given authority in our lives and we go forth to share that experience with our friends and neighbors.

As we prepare for Easter, may we, like the disciples, fall facedown in worship of the one who has been revealed as Lord of all.

PRAYER

Reread the story of the transfiguration. Reflect on the story in silence for a few moments.

God, thank you for revealing yourself to us in the person of Jesus. Help us to see the ways in which you have revealed yourself to us in our own lives and give us the courage to share those stories. Amen.

STANDARDS

"'What is it you want?' he asked. She said, 'Grant that one of these two sons of mine may sit at your right and the other at your left in your kingdom.'"

Read
Matthew 20:20-28

As a graduate student, I took a Latin course on the Roman historian Sallust. Most of my classmates were graduate students in the classics department, but a couple of students from the history department joined us as well. When it came time to translate and dialogue about the text, the standards by which we asked our questions were different. The historians were interested in times, locations, and people. The classicists were more interested in grammatical and rhetorical concerns.

In today's text, the mother of James and John, Salome, approaches Jesus with a very human question: she wants to see her sons put into a position of authority in Jesus' coming kingdom. What she does not realize is that she and Jesus operate under two very different standards of authority. Her standard is one of honor and achievement. Her sons have been following Jesus for almost three years now and they seem to be part of his inner circle. Don't they deserve a place of special honor? Jesus' standard, however, is not based on merit or ability. Rather, those who receive special honor are those who have made themselves servants to others.

It's easy to be hard on the mother of James and John. In a pious tone, we think to ourselves, "How dare she ask such a thing?" We think that we would never dare ask Jesus such a favor.

Yet all too often, like Salome, we hold Jesus to human standards. We think that following Jesus should mean a life of success, a life of health, or a life of easy living. We wonder why we face adversity. We look around and wonder why it seems that bad things always happen to good people. We hold Jesus to our standards.

But Jesus operates on different standards. Jesus operates on the standards of the kingdom. Jesus operates on the standards of love. Jesus operates on the standards of sacrificial living.

Whose standards will we live by?

PRAYER

Reflect on the ways in which we hold Jesus to human standards of what we expect from him.

God, forgive us for those times when we expect you to respond to us in accordance with our standards instead of yours. Help us to live under the standards of the kingdom. Amen.

KING

"This took place to fulfill what was spoken through the prophet."

Read Matthew 21:1-11

Palm Sunday presents a bit of an annual quandary for the church. Sermons on Palm Sunday tend to oscillate between two extremes. On the one hand, we celebrate that the people proclaim Jesus as King. We wave palm branches, our children shout "Hosanna!" and the mood is generally festive and happy.

On the other hand, we're often reminded that "Hosanna" is a politically motivated term and that the people are hoping for revolution. They are proclaiming Jesus as King because they think that he is going to overthrow the Roman government. We're told that the "triumphal entry" wasn't so triumphal after all.

While both sides contain aspects of the truth, I wonder if we somehow miss the point of Palm Sunday. The point isn't that the people misunderstand Jesus' political intentions. The point isn't whether the people "get it."

The point is that Jesus *is* King.

Whether the people understood it, even if they had the wrong idea of what Jesus was going to do, doesn't really matter.

What matters is that the King is riding through the gates of Jerusalem.

What matters is that Jesus is Lord.

What matters is that he is the rightful ruler of all of creation.

Throughout this past week we have encountered many of the ways in which we have false expectations of Jesus. We've seen the ways in which we hold Jesus to our own standards instead of letting him hold us to his.

On Palm Sunday, it's not our false expectations and incorrect standards that matter. What matters is that Jesus is King. And the King has come to his rightful kingdom.

Will we bow down and worship?

PRAYER

Shout "Hosanna!" today. If you can find a palm branch, wave it. Raise your hands in celebration of the King of all. Worship God with all of your heart and soul today and every day.

Jesus, thank you for revealing yourself to us as King. Help us to abandon ourselves in worship of you. Amen.

FIG

"Early in the morning, as Jesus was on his way back to the city, he was hungry."

Read
Matthew 21:12-22

Last Monday, when we first encountered Jesus, we met him after forty days without food and learned that he was hungry. We spent the last week encountering the man who was more than a man, the person who was no ordinary person.

Today, we find Jesus hungry once more.

He rides into Jerusalem and demonstrates his kingship. He clears the temple courts of those who have made it into a shopping mall. And then he's hungry.

So he finds the nearest fig tree, reaches out for a ripe, juicy fruit, only to realize that the tree has no fruit. So he curses the tree.

He curses the tree?

People everywhere begin to mutter things like "petty" and "mean-spirited." Why would Jesus curse a tree?

But then we go back to the night before, back to the temple, back to where the religious leaders of Jesus' day have made their faith into a financial transaction rather than a participation in God's covenant.

We realize that the fig tree isn't just a fig tree, and the figs aren't just figs.

There are trees that look like fig trees but do not act as fig trees. And there are people who look like the covenant people of God but do not live as covenant people of God.

And Jesus will have nothing to do with such trees.

If Jesus visited our churches this week, what would he find? Would he find vibrant life spilling over from covenantal relationship with God? Would he find lives being transformed and people coming to know God? Would he find a people laying God's covenant as the foundation of their academic pursuits, their career paths, and their family life?

Or would he find a place where people come to church only because they "have to," a place where we functionally exclude those who are different from us, a place where the pursuit of financial stability trumps a willingness to follow God?

There are trees that look like fig trees but do not act as fig trees. What about your life and your church?

PRAYER

How would Jesus respond if he visited your church? If he followed your life for a week?

God, help us to be people who think, love, and live as you would have us do. Help us to bear your fruit in every aspect of our lives. Amen.

WEDDING

"Therefore keep watch, because you do not know the day or the hour."

Read
Matthew 25:1-13

In today's reading, Jesus tells a story about a wedding for which people have waited a long time. It's the last days before the wedding and the excitement is growing.

In Jesus' day, a wedding would be announced long before it happened. Everyone waited for the day that the bridegroom came to get his bride, but they didn't know exactly when it would happen.

Finally, the groom comes for his bride, but not everyone is ready. Some thought that they had more time. They aren't prepared and run out of time to get the things they need. And so they're left out of the wedding. There's a feast and they're not there. They got tired of waiting and as a result they miss the excitement of the wedding.

Christians often struggle with the idea of Jesus' return. It's been two thousand years; why hasn't he returned yet? Jesus didn't return yesterday, he didn't return today, and my guess is that he won't return tomorrow, so why should I "keep watch"? I suspect that there are many of us who, even though we profess that Jesus will come again, believe this rather half-heartedly. Maybe some of us aren't even sure we would want Jesus to return tomorrow.

We've lost some of our anticipation for the wedding.

In Matthew 24, Jesus tells of the signs of the end times. Signs like wars, famines, and earthquakes. Signs that we see all around us.

There's going to be a wedding soon. It might be today. It might be tomorrow. It might be a year from now. It might even be a century (or ten) from now. But there's going to be a wedding soon.

The question is, how will we respond?

Will our excitement for the coming wedding spill over into every aspect of our lives? Will we tell everyone we know about the wedding that the whole world has been waiting for since the very dawn of creation?

Or will we tire of waiting? There's going to be a wedding soon.

PRAYER

What comes to mind when you think of Jesus' return? What does it look like to wait for Jesus' return with excitement and vigilance?

God, help us to wait for the day of your return with vigilance. Help us to share the excitement we have for the coming wedding between Christ and his church with everyone we know. Help us to do our best to put the name of Jesus on every aspect of our lives. Amen.

JUDAS

"Then one of the twelve—the one called Judas Iscariot—went to the chief priests and asked, 'What are you willing to give me if I deliver him over to you?'"

Read
Matthew 26:1-16

Most of us have experienced the pain of betrayal at some point in our lives. A friend who passes along hurtful gossip behind our backs. A coworker who intentionally stands in our way of success. The sting of rejection as our loved ones choose to love themselves more than us.

Today, we read two contrasting stories. The first is of a woman who chooses to use an expensive bottle of perfume to anoint Jesus. She gives from what she has in order to show honor to Jesus. And then, we have Judas. Judas' response to this act of love and devotion is to go and sell out Jesus to the chief priests.

Maybe he was sick of seeing Jesus "waste" money. Maybe he thought that Jesus was going to drive out the Romans and got tired of waiting. Maybe he was just plain greedy.

He chooses himself. He chooses *his* way. He sets his priorities and Jesus doesn't top the list.

Today and every day, we face the choice: whose way will we choose? Will we choose to love Jesus first and foremost or will we love ourselves? Will we choose our money, our positions, our careers, our learning, our families, our friends, our status, or anything else over our Lord and Savior Jesus?

We face the same choice that Judas faced. When Jesus doesn't live up to our expectations, how will we respond? Will we choose to put our own priorities and our own desires first? Or will we choose to love Jesus more than ourselves?

PRAYER

What things do you tend to put ahead of Jesus?

God, help us to love you first and foremost. Help us to choose to put you first this day and every day. Amen.

WONDER

"When they had sung a hymn, they went out to the Mount of Olives."

Read Matthew 26:17-30

Have you ever had one of those moments when something extraordinary happens? Something shakes you to your core, and you feel as though you have witnessed something simply amazing, and then you are shocked that the rest of the world continues on as though nothing has happened. Maybe it was the loss of a loved one or a medical diagnosis with no positive outlook. The world goes on and we're left standing in place, wondering how people can go about their daily business. Or perhaps it was something stunningly positive—the return of an estranged friend or an unexpected success at work or school. You find yourself overwhelmed by joy and are amazed to meet people who don't share your excitement.

I wonder sometimes how the disciples responded on this night, the night of the Last Supper. They were celebrating the Passover meal, an annual religious holiday. The disciples would know what was coming. As many of us have annual traditions at Thanksgiving or Christmas, the Jewish people had a set pattern of practices for celebrating

Passover. Jesus' proclamations in the middle of the Passover meal would have been unexpected and extraordinary. They likely would have shaken the disciples to the very core.

When the meal is over, Jesus returns to normal. He and the disciples sing a hymn as would be normal for the Passover meal. They go out to the Mount of Olives.

How did the disciples respond? What was it like for them to go from this extraordinary moment at the Passover meal back to the outside world? What thoughts raced through their minds as they walked in silence up the Mount of Olives?

Many of us will attend a Maundy Thursday service this evening to celebrate this Passover meal. As we encounter this moment in the night, the moment when Jesus makes an extraordinary pronouncement about who he is and what he is about to do, may we be overwhelmed by the moment. Whether or not we attend a Maundy Thursday service, may Jesus' words to his disciples shake us to our very core and assure us that we have witnessed something simply amazing.

As we return to our daily lives, may we bring with us the wonder and awe of the work of Jesus on the cross.

PRAYER

When was the last time you felt overwhelmed with wonder and awe as you celebrated the Lord's Supper?

Jesus, help us to encounter you today in an extraordinary and awe-inspiring way. Help us to bring our awe and wonder at the work of the cross with us into the rest of our lives. Amen.

IRONY

"Above his head they placed the written charge against him: THIS IS JESUS, THE KING OF THE JEWS."

Read
Matthew 27:32-56

Ironic, isn't it? Jesus is crucified and the mocking charge above his head is completely true.

But the truth is bigger than this sign. And, of course, it's not true in the way Jesus' accusers thought.

Yet it's a striking picture. On Good Friday we see Jesus, the true King, hanging on a cross—and in case we didn't know, there's a sign to tell us: this is Jesus, the King of the Jews.

On Good Friday we see what true divine love looks like. We see what true kingship looks like. On Good Friday we find that the King is the one who has been beaten and mocked, giving up his spirit for all people.

The sign is true, but the truth is bigger than this sign. Good Friday isn't just about the death of the King. Good Friday isn't even just about the forgiveness of sins, or about earning salvation for you and me, or even about making it possible to have a personal relationship with God.

Good Friday is the story of divine love. The story of a man who loves his bride so much that he would lay down his own life in order that she might find life. Good Friday is about more than you or me or any single one of us.

It's the story of God suffering and dying in order to conquer sin and death.

It's the story of Jesus openly showing that he is the King and offering us the chance to acknowledge his authority.

It's the story of Father, Son, and Holy Spirit reconciling the world to the triune God.

It's the story of love waiting to declare its victory on Sunday morning, as the world waits with bated breath for the stone to be rolled back on Easter.

PRAYER

Pause for a few minutes to reflect on this weekend, the climax to the divine love story of God and the world.

God, thank you for what you did on the cross. Help us to never lose our wonder and amazement at the suffering you underwent for our sake. Help the cross never to become "old news" but to strike us again and again with wonder. Amen.

TOMB

> "So give the order for the tomb to be made secure until the third day. Otherwise, his disciples may come and steal the body and tell the people that he has been raised from the dead."
>
> **Read** Matthew 27:57-66

If you ask people what they believe about Jesus, my guess is that most will fall somewhere along this continuum of reasoning:

1. Jesus is a made-up character who never actually existed. (Except that the existence of a prominent first-century Jewish Messiah figure named Jesus is well-documented in other literature.)
2. There was a real Jesus but he was just an ordinary man who achieved some prominence and was killed for stirring a potential revolution. (Except that the gospels record many things that Jesus did that are beyond ordinary.)
3. There was a real Jesus who did some extraordinary things and his followers, so distraught by his death, exaggerated the things Jesus said and attributed to him miracles that didn't really happen. (Except that of the remaining eleven disciples, all except John died as martyrs, rather than deny the truth of the gospel.)

4. There was a real Jesus who did everything recorded about him in the gospels, was crucified on a cross, and rose again from the dead. He truly was the Son of God.

Extrabiblical sources and archaeological records can only take us so far. At some point, everyone must face a critical question: will we trust that the gospels faithfully represent the reality of Jesus' life?

As we wait for Easter morning and as the world accuses the disciples of making it all up, we celebrate the victory of the cross. We find our hearts transformed by Jesus' love demonstrated for us on Good Friday. We proclaim the lordship of Christ announced on Easter morning.

Rational argument can only go so far. At some point, we need the Spirit of God working in our hearts to convict us of the truth of the gospels. In the words of an old song, "You ask me how I know he lives, he lives within my heart."

May we declare the good news of Easter again today and every day.

PRAYER

Think about your friends and neighbors. Who do they think Jesus is? Have you ever asked them?

God, thank you for your work on the cross. In this time of year when many are open to attending Easter worship services, we pray that you would open their hearts to your gospel message. We pray for our friends and neighbors who do not yet know Jesus. Amen.

GO

"Therefore go and make disciples of all nations, baptizing them in the name of the Father and of the Son and of the Holy Spirit, and teaching them to obey everything I have commanded you. And surely I am with you always, to the very end of the age."

Read Matthew 28:1-20

At last we have arrived. Forty-six days. Forty-six days to reflect on our need for the Savior. Forty-six days to prepare for this day.

Over the last several weeks, we have encountered God's people as they prepared to do God's work.

The last six Sundays, we have seen foreshadowing of the message of Easter, miniature reminders in the midst of the somber mood of Lent of the celebration for which we were waiting.

Today at last we have reached the celebration. At last we have arrived at the resurrection.

And then Matthew does something interesting. A few short sentences later, he's done. He references the doubt of some of the disciples, but that's about it. No road to Emmaus, no miraculous catch of fish, no reinstatement of Peter, as we see in the other gospels. Instead, Jesus' command: make disciples of all nations. The Greek word for "go" here is a participle and could properly be translated "As you go." The command is simple: As you go, make disciples.

The glory of Easter is simply too much to be contained. The joy of the resurrection cannot be kept silent. The message of the gospel overcomes all doubt and all skepticism, and we have the privilege to share in the process of making disciples.

When we go to church: Make disciples.

When we go to school: Make disciples.

When we go to work: Make disciples.

When we're eating lunch: Make disciples.

It sounds like something we encountered a few weeks ago in Deuteronomy: "Talk about them when you sit at home and when you walk along the road, when you lie down and when you get up" (Deuteronomy 6:4).

Wherever we go and whatever we do, the message of Easter morning is on our lips, proclaiming the good news for all people everywhere to hear:

He is risen! He is risen indeed. Amen.

PRAYER

Enjoy this Easter Sunday. Proclaim with joy that Christ is risen. Celebrate the new life we have in Christ. Share the good news of the gospel wherever you go.

Father, Son, and Holy Spirit, on this day, the day when we celebrate your victory over sin and death, the day when we rejoice again in your salvation, fill us with an excitement for the gospel that cannot be contained. Amen.